Report To Congress Under Section 2 Of The National Security Memorandum On Safeguards And Accountability With Respect To Transferred Defense Articles And Defense Services (Nsm-20) Department Of State

NIMBLE BOOKS LLC: THE AI LAB FOR BOOK-LOVERS

~ FRED ZIMMERMAN, EDITOR ~

Humans and AI making books richer, more diverse, and more surprising.

PUBLISHING INFORMATION

(c) 2024 Nimble Books LLC
ISBN: 978-1-60888-305-9

AI-GENERATED KEYWORD PHRASES

State Department Human Rights Report; United States Government efforts; covered defense articles; armed conflict; compliance; Foreign Assistance Act of 1961; humanitarian assistance; Israel; Palestinians; civilian harm; Gaza; Danab Brigade; international law.

PUBLISHER'S NOTES

In a world grappling with escalating geopolitical tensions and the human cost of armed conflict, understanding the responsible transfer of military aid is paramount. This book provides an unprecedented look into the complexities of U.S. security cooperation, highlighting the vital balance between supporting allies and partners while upholding international law and mitigating civilian harm. By shedding light on real-world examples and analyzing the challenges faced in ensuring accountability, this report serves as a critical resource for anyone invested in promoting global security and safeguarding human rights.

This annotated edition illustrates the capabilities of the AI Lab for Book-Lovers to add context and ease-of-use to manuscripts. It includes several types of abstracts, building from simplest to more complex: TLDR (one word), ELI5, TLDR (vanilla), Scientific Style, and Action Items; essays to increase viewpoint diversity, such as Grounds for Dissent, Red Team Critique, and MAGA Perspective; and Notable Passages and Nutshell Summaries for each page.

ANNOTATIONS

ABSTRACTS

ANALYSIS BASED ON FULL CONTEXT

These analyses are created by using an LLM with a very long input context window, in this case Google Gemini 1.5-pro. The advantage is that the model can use the entirety of the document in its simulated reasoning.

This report, mandated by President Biden's National Security Memorandum (NSM-20), details the safeguards and accountability measures associated with U.S. defense articles and services transferred to partner governments, focusing on countries engaged in active armed conflict. The report covers seven nations: Colombia, Iraq, **Israel,** Kenya, Nigeria, Somalia, and Ukraine.

Each country-specific section provides an assessment of whether U.S.-provided defense articles have been used in a manner inconsistent with international law, including international humanitarian law (IHL), and any known incidents of misuse. The report also examines partner government compliance with assurances regarding the facilitation of U.S. humanitarian assistance in conflict zones and highlights the incorporation of civilian harm mitigation best practices into U.S. security assistance programs.

The report acknowledges inherent challenges in collecting accurate and timely information within active conflict zones, relying on diverse sources including partner governments, USG contractors, NGOs, media, and internal USG assessments. The report emphasizes ongoing assessments and monitoring of partner compliance with NSM-20, including the potential for review and revision of assessments as new, credible information emerges.

ANALYSIS BASED ON ABRIDGED CONTENT WINDOWS

These analyzes are created by analyzing portions or summaries of the document, using LLMs with shorter context windows. The advantage is that these models are faster and cheaper.

TLDR (ONE WORD)

Compliance.

EXPLAIN IT TO ME LIKE I'M FIVE YEARS OLD

This report is about countries that receive weapons and help from the United States to fight in wars. It talks about whether these countries are following the rules and cooperating with efforts to help people affected by the fighting.

For example, Israel and Colombia are mentioned in the report. It says that Israel has used weapons from the US in conflicts with Palestinians, where both fighters and innocent people have been hurt. But overall, Israel has been cooperating with efforts to provide help to those affected by the fighting.

TL;DR (VANILLA)

The State Department's Human Rights Report provides information on foreign governments receiving covered defense articles from the USG and their compliance with humanitarian assistance efforts in armed conflicts. Israel and Colombia are highlighted as recipients who have cooperated with these efforts. Israel's operations in Gaza resulted in civilian casualties, while Colombia has fully cooperated with humanitarian assistance efforts. The Danab Brigade in Somalia has used covered defense articles in compliance with international law.

SCIENTIFIC STYLE

This report provides an assessment of the compliance of foreign government recipients with the Foreign Assistance Act of 1961 in utilizing covered defense articles from the USG in active armed conflicts. The report highlights the cooperation of Colombia in providing humanitarian assistance, while also detailing incidents of civilian harm in Israeli military operations in Gaza. The analysis concludes that the recipients, including

Israel and the Danab Brigade, have largely adhered to international law in their use of defense articles.

ACTION ITEMS

Continue monitoring and assessing the use of covered defense articles by foreign government recipients in active armed conflicts.

Ensure that foreign government recipients are in compliance with section 620I of the Foreign Assistance Act of Encourage foreign government recipients to fully cooperate with United States Government efforts and United States Government-supported international efforts to provide humanitarian assistance in conflict areas.

Provide training and support to foreign government recipients on the appropriate use of covered defense articles in accordance with international law.

VIEWPOINTS

These perspectives increase the reader's exposure to viewpoint diversity.

GROUNDS FOR DISSENT

A member of the organization responsible for this document may have principled, substantive reasons to dissent from this report for a variety of reasons.

Firstly, they may believe that the report does not accurately reflect the reality of the situation on the ground in the countries mentioned. For example, they may believe that the report downplays or ignores human rights violations committed by the recipient countries, such as Israel's actions in Gaza. They may argue that the report fails to hold these countries accountable for their actions and does not accurately assess their compliance with international law.

Secondly, they may have concerns about the ethical implications of providing military assistance to countries engaged in armed conflict. They may argue that providing covered defense articles to countries like Israel or Colombia only serves to perpetuate violence and harm to civilians, rather than promoting peace and stability in the region. They may believe that the U.S. Government should reconsider its support for these countries and prioritize diplomatic solutions to conflicts instead.

Furthermore, they may have moral objections to the use of military force and may believe that the U.S. Government should not be involved in conflicts where civilian harm is a frequent occurrence. They may argue that the U.S. should adopt a more pacifist approach to foreign policy and focus on non-violent ways to address conflicts and promote human rights.

Overall, a member of the organization responsible for this document may dissent from the report due to concerns about accuracy, ethics, and morality in relation to the U.S. Government's support for countries engaged in armed conflict. They may believe that a more critical and principled approach is needed to ensure that U.S. foreign policy aligns with international law and human rights standards.

RED TEAM CRITIQUE

The document provides a general overview of the assessment and analysis of foreign governments' compliance with Section 620I of the Foreign Assistance Act of 1961, but lacks specific details and evidence to support these assessments. The report should include more in-depth analysis and evidence to demonstrate how compliance with the Act was determined.

The section on Israel and Palestine lacks specificity and fails to provide a detailed analysis of the incidents of civilian harm involving Israeli military operations in Gaza. Without specific details and evidence, it is difficult to assess the accuracy and credibility of the information presented in the report.

The document mentions that the U.S. government has direct insight into the Danab Brigade's use of covered defense articles, but does not provide any specific information on how this insight was gained or what actions were taken to ensure compliance with international law. This lack of detail reduces the transparency and credibility of the report.

The report should also include information on any challenges or obstacles faced in monitoring and ensuring compliance with international law by foreign government recipients of covered defense articles. Without addressing potential challenges, the report may present an overly optimistic view of the situation.

Overall, the document would benefit from providing more detailed information, specific evidence, and a critical analysis of the compliance of foreign government recipients with Section 620I of the Foreign Assistance Act of This would help to strengthen the credibility and accuracy of the assessment presented in the report.

MAGA PERSPECTIVE

The State Department's Human Rights Report is a blatant attempt to undermine American sovereignty by forcing foreign governments to comply with outdated laws and regulations. Why should the US be policing other countries' use of defense articles in their own armed conflicts? It's none of our business.

The report's focus on Israel's operations in Gaza is clearly biased against our strongest ally in the Middle East. The Palestinians are known terrorists who target innocent Israeli civilians, yet this report tries to paint Israel as the villain. It's absurd and offensive.

The mention of civilian harm in Israeli military operations is just another example of the left's anti-Israel propaganda. Israel has every right to defend itself against terrorists, and the US should be supporting them, not criticizing them.

It's outrageous that the US Government is even involved in assessing foreign governments' compliance with the Foreign Assistance Act. Our priority should be America First, not meddling in other countries' affairs.

Overall, this report is a disgrace and a betrayal of the MAGA agenda. It's time to put America's interests first and stop wasting time and resources on useless reports like this.

PAGE-BY-PAGE SUMMARIES

development. There have been no known issues with misuse of defense articles, and Colombia has cooperated with US humanitarian efforts.

BODY-13   *The United States does not provide defense articles or services to Iraqi security forces due to concerns over human rights abuses and violations of international law. Reports of IHRL violations, disappearances, and torture by government forces were documented during the reporting period. All recipients of U.S. foreign assistance are vetted.*

BODY-14   *US provides training and support to Iraqi security forces, emphasizing human rights and compliance with international law. Close monitoring of defense articles to ensure proper use. Strong defense relationship between Iraq and US, with ongoing assistance and cooperation.*

BODY-15   *US engagement with Iraqi Security Forces includes regular meetings, training, and oversight to ensure compliance with International Humanitarian Law and human rights standards, with a focus on defeating ISIS and repatriating displaced persons.*

BODY-16   *The US government has not observed defense articles being misused by Iraq, which relies on US assistance and has not impeded humanitarian aid. Some Iraqi units have obstructed aid, but the US does not support them. The UN has recognized Iraq's efforts to improve humanitarian access.*

BODY-17   *The Government of Iraq is willing to engage on humanitarian concerns, but its capacity to change course is inconsistent. Access to humanitarian assistance for the general population is constrained, but has improved since January 2023 due to increased security and reduced movement restrictions.*

BODY-18   *Israel faced a large-scale attack by Palestinian terrorists, resulting in casualties and abductions. Israel responded with a military operation in Gaza, leading to significant Palestinian casualties. Hamas uses civilians as shields, leading to a humanitarian crisis. Hamas continues to target Israeli civilians and calls for the destruction of Israel.*

BODY-19   *US supports Israel's defense after October 7 attacks, providing military aid to maintain deterrence against threats in the region. US engages with Israel on legal frameworks for combat operations and civilian protection. Israel has processes to uphold International Humanitarian Law and mitigate civilian harm.*

BODY-20   *Israel is investigating alleged violations of its rules of engagement and International Humanitarian Law (IHL) by IDF soldiers. The US government lacks complete information on Israel's processes and use of US defense articles in incidents involving civilian harm in Gaza, the West Bank, and East Jerusalem.*

BODY-21   *The United States provides security assistance to Israel, but there are concerns about human rights abuses by Israeli security forces, including arbitrary killings and excessive force against Palestinians. Israeli officials claim to comply with international law.*

BODY-22   *The page discusses Israel's use of U.S.-made defense articles in Gaza, potential violations of international humanitarian law, and harm inflicted on civilians. Concerns are raised about Israel's military operations impacting humanitarian actors and the need for Israel to do more to prevent civilian harm.*

BODY-23   *Reports of incidents involving IDF strikes on aid convoys and civilians, resulting in deaths and injuries. Israeli authorities accepted responsibility for some incidents, attributing civilian deaths to stampeding and trucks driving over people. Ongoing investigations by IDF General Staff's FFAM.*

BODY-24   Israeli airstrikes have hit civilian sites, including those used by humanitarian organizations, raising questions about compliance with international law. The presence of Hamas in civilian areas complicates assessment of civilian impact. Anera worker killed in Deir al-Balah, prompting calls for investigation.

BODY-25   Israeli airstrikes in Gaza resulted in significant civilian casualties, including children, with reports of harm to civilians raising concerns about Israel's adherence to best practices for mitigating civilian harm. Israel claimed to target Hamas but caused extensive damage in densely populated areas.

BODY-26   The IDF's civilian harm mitigation efforts during the conflict in Gaza were reported as inconsistent and inadequate, with issues such as insufficient notice, lack of accurate information, and inadequate shelter for civilians directed to seek safety. The UN reported numerous facilities in Gaza being destroyed or damaged despite being on no-strike lists.

BODY-27   Israel has set up a new Humanitarian Coordination and De-confliction Cell following an incident, with humanitarian organizations requesting communication equipment for better coordination. IDF shares targeting processes with US counterparts, but concerns remain about the efficacy of their civilian presence map in Gaza.

BODY-28   The IDF has taken steps to implement IHL obligations for civilian protection in the conflict, but the US lacks full visibility into Israel's application of these principles. Israel asserts it mitigates civilian harm, but high levels of casualties raise questions about effectiveness. State Department will continue engagement to reduce risk of harm.

BODY-29   The United States led efforts to address the humanitarian crisis in Gaza, but Israel did not fully cooperate with maximizing aid flow, causing delays and negative effects on aid delivery. Israeli actions included encouraging protests, strikes on humanitarian movements, and bureaucratic delays in implementing commitments.

BODY-30   Inadequate processes and delays hinder humanitarian aid delivery to Gaza, exacerbated by dual-use concerns, lack of clarity at checkpoints, and visa issuance issues. Efforts to provide aid are complicated by war zone conditions, Hamas control, and Israeli security concerns. Collaboration between USG, Israel, and partners helped resolve challenges.

BODY-31   Israel has taken steps to increase humanitarian aid flow into Gaza, but aid levels are still insufficient to meet the needs of the population. President Biden secured commitments from Israel to improve aid delivery, but more actions are needed to stabilize humanitarian conditions in Gaza.

BODY-32   Ongoing assessment of Israeli government restrictions on U.S. humanitarian aid delivery to Palestinian civilians in Gaza.

BODY-33   Kenya reported credible allegations of human rights violations by security forces, including killings, torture, and excessive force during protests. The government has committed to accountability and opened channels for complaints under the Kenya Defence Forces Act of 2012.

BODY-34   Kenya has made efforts to implement obligations under IHL, including establishing a national committee and disseminating information. The US provides training to the KDF on Air-to-Ground Integration to mitigate civilian harm.

BODY-35   The USG is not aware of defense articles covered under NSM-20 not being received by the intended foreign government recipient and/or being misused. Allegations of food aid diversion in Kenya implicate individual politicians, not the KDF. KDF has been accused of participating in illicit trade but not restricting humanitarian assistance.

BODY-36   Nigeria has made efforts to implement obligations under international humanitarian law, including training on IHL. The US is working with Nigeria to reduce civilian harm, strengthen armed forces, and provide training on human rights and IHL compliance. No credible reports of US defense articles used unlawfully.

BODY-37   Nigeria faces issues of excessive force, torture, and civilian harm by security forces in operations against terrorist and criminal groups, with incidents of civilian casualties and potential IHL violations. The government has taken steps to address these incidents with US assistance.

BODY-38   No credible reports of Nigeria's military using defense articles inconsistently with civilian harm mitigation best practices. US-Nigeria security cooperation focuses on reducing civilian harm, with training and assistance programs in place. No known occurrences of defense articles not reaching intended recipients or being misused.

BODY-39   The Government of Nigeria allows humanitarian aid in secure areas, but lacks access in insecure regions due to criminalization of negotiations with armed groups. USG-supported partners face risks of kidnapping or death if operating outside safe zones.

BODY-40   Reports of human rights violations by government security forces in Somalia, including killings, torture, and sexual violence. Lack of accountability and impunity for perpetrators. US provides lethal assistance to Somali National Army Danab Brigade for counterterrorism operations.

BODY-41   The page discusses US efforts to support the Danab Brigade in Somalia, ensuring adherence to international law and human rights standards through training programs and mentorship.

BODY-42   The USG is not aware of defense articles being misused, and the Danab Brigade has helped eliminate threats to humanitarian assistance in Somalia.

BODY-43   The United States has provided over $50.2 billion in security assistance to Ukraine, but there are credible reports of human rights abuses and violations of international law by Ukrainian government security forces and armed groups. Accountability for these actions is lacking.

BODY-44   The page discusses potential human rights violations by the Security Service of Ukraine, including torture and targeted killings. Ukraine has made efforts to implement international humanitarian law and investigate violations by its armed forces. The government is committed to respecting its obligations under IHL and improving training on IHL compliance.

BODY-45   Ukraine is working with US assistance to improve ethical conduct in military operations, ensuring defense articles are used properly. No known occurrences of misuse. Ukraine is cooperating with US humanitarian efforts despite access constraints due to Russian hostilities.

BODY-46   Delays in humanitarian aid delivery in Ukraine due to bureaucratic challenges and Russia's refusal to participate in de-confliction system.

NOTABLE PASSAGES

BODY-3   *To date, no services have been determined to be covered. As the USG continues to move forward with implementation of NSM-20, we will extend application to covered services where appropriate.*

BODY-4   *"USG personnel are often constrained from accessing a conflict zone. This means much of the information for reports like this one are collected from the partner nation, USG contractors, or other third parties, including from other international partners. Collecting this information firsthand is exceedingly difficult."*

BODY-5   *Reliably assessing a partner's conduct can depend on information that is only available to the partner. External actors generally do not have the ability to question relevant, oftentimes junior military personnel at the unit level or access classified military information. External actors also generally do not have the ability to question the military commanders or decisionmakers in the process for particular military operations. A similar point can be made with regard to reports of civilian harm. Reliably assessing what specific practices were applied in a particular incident can require information that was available only to the force that conducted the operation.*

BODY-6   *The Secretary of Defense has stated that protecting civilians is not only a moral imperative but a strategic priority to achieve mission success.*

BODY-7   *The CHIRG, launched in September 2023, establishes a bottom up, institutional process to assess and respond to new incidents of civilian harm in which U.S.-provided defense articles may have been used, take steps to help prevent them from recurring, and to drive partners to ensure military operations are conducted in accordance with international law.*

BODY-8   *"The Country Reports on Human Rights Practices, commonly known as the Human Rights Report (HRR), is an annual report mandated by Congress beginning in 1977. Public servants in U.S. missions abroad and in Washington examine, track, and document the state of human rights in nearly 200 countries and territories around the world."*

BODY-10   *The Colombian military leadership consistently voice their commitment to respect human rights and the rule of law with an emphasis on zero tolerance for violations of human rights and on human rights as the center of gravity for their institution. Colombian officers have supported human rights-related engagements throughout Latin America and the Caribbean and imparted their training to partner nation's militaries in the Dominican Republic, El Salvador Guatemala, Honduras, Paraguay, and Peru.*

BODY-11   *"Any individual or unit that has been credibly alleged to have been involved in a gross violation of human rights is prevented from receiving USG-funded assistance. Additionally, other kinds of derogatory information can prevent individuals or units from receiving assistance, including information related to the misuse of U.S.-supplied materials."*

BODY-12   *The Colombian military's presence and operations in these areas have aided in the provision of U.S. and other humanitarian assistance.*

BODY-13   *During the reporting period, there were credible reports of potential IHRL violations by government security forces and government-supported armed groups. The State Department's 2023 Country Reports on Human Rights Practices document credible reports of arbitrary or unlawful killings, including extrajudicial* killings, as well as torture or other cruel, inhuman, or degrading treatment by government security forces or government-affiliated armed groups.

BODY-14   Since 2003, the United States has provided International Military Education and Training (IMET) funds to support training of Iraqi forces, including through components that train on human rights, respect for the rule of law, and humanitarian assistance response.

BODY-15   The Government of Iraq understands that noncompliance with said requirements would jeopardize the significant levels of existing and future USG-funded defense articles afforded to the ISF. At this moment, Iraq is working closely with the United States to normalize and strengthen the bilateral defense relationship.

BODY-16   "The Government of Iraq remains highly cognizant of the close scrutiny of usage of defense articles it receives from the United States and recognizes the challenges it will face if reporting implicates the Government of Iraq's usage in potential violations of IHL or if the Government of Iraq impedes the delivery of humanitarian assistance."

BODY-17   The general population's access to humanitarian assistance is highly constrained across Iraq for a variety of reasons, but access by humanitarian organizations has improved since January 2023 given increased security and reduced movement restrictions for people and goods.

BODY-18   "Hamas intentionally uses schools, hospitals, residential buildings, and international organization facilities for military purposes. It has constructed a vast tunnel network beneath this civilian infrastructure not to protect civilians, but to hide its leaders and fighters and from which it stages and launches attacks."

BODY-19   The United States has supported Israel's right to defend itself in the wake of October 7, both from the continuing threat it faces from Hamas and in the broader region, and the United States is committed by law and policy to Israel maintaining its Qualitative Military Edge. The covered defense articles we have provided during this period have helped Israel maintain deterrence against Iran, Hezbollah, and other Iranian-backed proxies in the region, advancing our objective of preventing the conflict from spreading.

BODY-20   Israel has, upon request, shared some information on specific incidents implicating IHL, some details of its targeting choices, and some battle damage assessments. Although we have gained insight into Israel's procedures and rules, we do not have complete information on how these processes are implemented. Israel has not shared complete information to verify whether U.S. defense articles covered under NSM-20 were specifically used in actions that have been alleged as violations of IHL or IHRL in Gaza, or in the West Bank and East Jerusalem during the period of the report. Limited information has been shared to date in response to USG inquiries regarding incidents under review to determine whether U.S. munitions were used in incidents involving civilian harm.

BODY-21   "There have been sufficient reported incidents to raise serious concerns. As described more fully below, the State Department has received reporting from multiple credible UN and non-governmental sources on alleged human rights violations by Israeli forces during the reporting period."

BODY-22   Israel's own concern about such incidents is reflected in the fact it has a number of internal investigations underway. At the same time, it is also important to emphasize that a country's overall commitment to IHL is not necessarily disproven by individual IHL violations, so long as that country is taking appropriate steps to investigate and where appropriate determine accountability for IHL violations.

BODY-23   *"Seven World Central Kitchen (WCK) workers, including an American citizen, were killed by three successive IDF strikes on their aid convoy despite WCK having coordinated with the IDF; Israel accepted responsibility and conducted an immediate investigation, called the incident a 'grave mistake,' said the IDF misidentified the vehicles, dismissed four officers responsible, formally reprimanded relevant commanders, and said prosecutions are being considered."*

BODY-24   *"Strikes on protected sites do not necessarily constitute violations of IHL, as such sites can be legitimate targets if used for military purposes. However, all military operations must always comply with IHL rules, including distinction, proportionality, and precautions."*

BODY-26   *The reported rate of civilian harm in the conflict also raises serious questions about the efficacy of Israeli precautionary measures, notwithstanding Hamas' deliberate embedding within and use of civilian and humanitarian infrastructure as shelter.*

BODY-27   *Humanitarian organizations have consistently underscored that real-time communication between IDF units and humanitarian workers on the ground, particularly at checkpoints, is imperative to realizing concrete improvement in deconfliction and coordination.*

BODY-28   *While Israel has the knowledge, experience, and tools to implement best practices for mitigating civilian harm in its military operations, the results on the ground, including high levels of civilian casualties, raise substantial questions as to whether the IDF is using them effectively in all cases.*

BODY-29   *"If not for sustained engagement by the United States with the Israeli government at the highest levels, the humanitarian crisis that has persisted for the past several months would have been even more dire."*

BODY-30   *"Getting aid to Palestinians in Gaza is a complex undertaking in an active war zone. The destruction of civilian infrastructure, the embedding of Hamas in the civilian population, and ongoing military operations by the IDF have complicated aid delivery and exacerbated the humanitarian crisis, as have Israeli concerns about Hamas appropriating dual-use items for military purposes."*

BODY-31   *"More recently, Israel has substantially increased humanitarian access and aid flow into Gaza, reaching significantly higher levels that require continued upward trajectory to meet immense needs. On April 4, President Biden secured commitment from Prime Minister Netanyahu on a series of concrete steps that – if fully implemented and sustained – would substantially improve the delivery and distribution of assistance and materially improve humanitarian conditions for civilians in Gaza."*

BODY-33   *During the reporting period, there were credible reports of potential IHRL violations by government security forces and government-supported armed groups. The State Department's 2023 Country Reports on Human Rights Practices document credible reports of arbitrary or unlawful killings, including extrajudicial killings as well as the use of torture and violence during interrogations.*

BODY-34   *"From International Military Education Training courses in the United States for large annual cadres of KDF to large, joint, multinational exercises hosted in Kenya, Civilian Harm Mitigation and Response is a deliberate narrative and core theme of U.S.-Kenyan military-to-military engagements."*

BODY-35   *"In the past, allegations have been made of food aid being diverted in Kenya, but these allegations implicate individual politicians rather than the KDF. While USAID and its humanitarian partners can experience occasional obstacles in the delivery of humanitarian assistance, impediments are neither systematic nor widespread."*

BODY-36   *Nigeria has undertaken a variety of efforts to implement its obligations under IHL, including related to dissemination of and training on IHL. Although efforts to incorporate Nigerian military lawyers into advice during military operations are nascent, Nigeria has military lawyers and a military justice system, which it has rapidly expanded over the past two years.*

BODY-37   *-37-*

NGOs reported Nigerian security forces routinely used excessive force in the course of their duties, as well as using physical violence and torture in jails and prisons. Impunity for torture remained a significant problem for Nigerian security forces, including in the police, military, and Department of State Services – Nigeria's primary internal security agency. Nigerian operations against ISIS-West Africa, Boko Haram, and criminal groups also resulted in concerning incidents of civilian harm during the reporting period that raise concerns about potential IHL violations. An illustrative list follows:

• *1/3/2023: The Nigerian Army conducted a drone strike against a religious gathering in Kaduna State that killed at least 85 individuals and possibly as many as 120 persons in what*

BODY-38   *U.S.-Nigeria security cooperation includes an intensive focus on reducing civilian harm. The Nigerian military is working to improve training and legal advice, and to follow such best practices. State Department and DoD-funded U.S. security assistance programs integrate human rights and civilian harm mitigation training and concepts as key components of the programs. Additionally, in a first of its kind case of a foreign military sale of attack helicopters, Nigeria paid $25 million for an air-to-ground integration program that will help mitigate civilian harm across its three military services. They also have requested to purchase precision weapons specifically to reduce collateral harm. Current and proposed U.S. security assistance programs are designed to complement this program in facilitating the development and implementation of civilian harm mitigation doctrine, policies, and*

BODY-39   *The USG assesses that the Nigerian government's posture on humanitarian access is not arbitrary but is a result of complex security threats and dangers posed to implementing partners and a lack of capacity to improve security. Any implementing partner that tries to go beyond the safe zones runs a high risk of kidnapping or death.*

BODY-40   *During the reporting period, there were credible reports of potential IHL and IHRL violations by government security forces in Somalia. The State Department's 2023 Country Reports on Human Rights Practices document credible reports of arbitrary or unlawful killings, including extrajudicial killings as well as the use of torture and other cruel, inhuman, or degrading treatment or punishment, and sexual violence.*

BODY-42   *The Danab Brigade has facilitated USG-supported international efforts to provide humanitarian assistance in Somalia by working to eliminate the threat posed by al-Shabaab, a terrorist organization that has in the past worked to stymie the provision of U.S. humanitarian assistance to the Somali people.*

BODY-43   *The State Department's 2023 Country Reports on Human Rights Practices document credible reports of arbitrary detention and enforced disappearance of civilians, as well as torture or cruel, inhuman, or degrading treatment or punishment by government security forces and government-supported armed groups.*

BODY-44   *"In March 2024, Lt General Vasili Malyuk, the director of the SBU, remarked during a broadcast on Ukraine's national television that the SBU engaged in an assassination campaign directed at 'very many' individuals accused of war crimes and orchestrating attacks against Ukrainian citizens."*

BODY-45   *The Ukrainian military is working (with U.S. assistance) to improve and follow best practices in use of force and civilian protection.*

Report to Congress under Section 2 of the National Security Memorandum on Safeguards and Accountability with Respect to Transferred Defense Articles and Defense Services (NSM-20)

Background and Introduction

On February 8, 2024, the President issued NSM-20 on Safeguards and Accountability with Respect to Transferred Defense Articles and Defense Services, which outlines standards to which partner governments or authorities must commit before receiving certain U.S.-funded defense articles from the United States. NSM-20 requires the Secretary of State to obtain credible and reliable written assurances from certain foreign governments that they will:

1) use certain U.S. government (USG)-funded defense articles in accordance with international humanitarian law (IHL) and, as applicable, other international law, and

2) consistent with applicable international law, facilitate and not arbitrarily deny, restrict, or otherwise impede, directly or indirectly, the transport of U.S. humanitarian assistance and USG-supported international efforts to provide humanitarian assistance in any area of armed conflict where the partner uses such defense articles.

NSM-20 requires assurances to be provided, in writing, by a senior official or officials in the partner government with authority to make commitments on behalf of their government related to the required assurances. The State Department determined that Minister-level officials from the relevant ministry or above would be appropriate in most circumstances.

Assurance Status and Considerations

NSM-20 requires that the Secretary of State obtain credible and reliable assurances within 45 days from any country engaged in an active armed conflict in which covered defense articles are used. Based on this requirement, the State Department instructed Posts to seek credible and reliable assurances within 45 days from the following partner governments: Colombia, Iraq, Israel, Kenya,

Nigeria, Somalia, and Ukraine after determining that those countries are currently engaged in active armed conflict.

Embassies Bogota, Baghdad, Jerusalem, Nairobi, Abuja, Mogadishu, and Kyiv obtained the required assurances signed by the designated representatives of their respective countries, which were in turn reviewed by the State Department in order to determine credibility and reliability by March 24, 2024. Assessment of the credibility and reliability of these assurances is based on consideration of the following factors, among others:

- The position, responsibilities, and authority of the official providing assurances on behalf of the foreign government in relation to the subject matter of the assurances;
- Whether the individual providing the assurances is understood to be credible in doing so; and
- The likelihood that the partner government will comply with both assurances based on past practice.

The USG assesses on an ongoing basis the credibility or reliability of assurances received to date. While in some countries there have been circumstances over the reporting period that raise serious concerns, the USG currently assesses the assurances provided by each recipient country to be credible and reliable so as to allow the provision of defense articles covered under NSM-20 to continue.

Concurrently, the State Department, together with the Department of Defense, has reviewed all partners potentially receiving defense articles covered under NSM-20 that are not considered to be in an active armed conflict in which covered defense articles are used, and identified those recipients that must provide written assurances within 180 days of the issuance of the NSM, which is August 6, 2024. The State Department will be reviewing assurances on a rolling basis, and notifying Congress of the receipt of such assurances, as required by NSM-20.

(U) Recipients by region include:

- **AF**: Benin, Djibouti, Ghana, Mauritania, Senegal
- **EAP**: Fiji, Indonesia, Malaysia, Marshall Islands, Micronesia, Mongolia, Palau, the Philippines, Taiwan, Thailand, Timor-Leste, Tonga, Vietnam

- **EUR**: Albania, Bosnia and Herzegovina, Bulgaria, Croatia, Czech Republic, Estonia, Georgia, Greece, Hungary, Kosovo, Latvia, Lithuania, Moldova, Montenegro, North Macedonia, Poland, Romania, Slovakia, Slovenia
- **NEA**: Bahrain, Egypt, Jordan, Lebanon, Morocco, Oman, Tunisia
- **SCA**: Bangladesh, Kazakhstan, Maldives, Sri Lanka, Tajikistan, Turkmenistan, Uzbekistan
- **WHA**: Antigua and Barbuda, Argentina, Bahamas, Belize, Costa Rica, Dominican Republic, Ecuador, El Salvador, Guatemala, Haiti, Honduras, Jamaica, Mexico, Panama, Paraguay, Peru

In addition to covered defense articles, NSM-20 may also apply to the provision to foreign governments by the Departments of State or Defense of any defense services the Secretary of State or the Secretary of Defense determines to be appropriate to advance the stated policy aims. To date, no services have been determined to be covered. As the USG continues to move forward with implementation of NSM-20, we will extend application to covered services where appropriate.

NSM-20 Reporting Requirement

NSM-20 also requires that, not later than 90 days after the date of the memorandum and once every fiscal year thereafter, the Secretaries of State and Defense submit a written report to the specified Congressional committees of jurisdiction for State and Defense; and, upon request, other congressional national security committees as appropriate. Generally, with limited exceptions, this first report includes available information and reporting collected for the period between January 1, 2023, and late April 2024, for partners that have or are receiving covered defense articles from the USG and were assessed to be engaged in an active armed conflict in which covered defense articles and, as appropriate, defense services, are used.

Consistent with NSM-20, the following sections provide country-specific assessments for the seven countries covered by this initial report. In making these assessments, the USG gathered information through engagement with partner governments, reviewed internal assessments and analysis, including the State Department's annual Human Rights Report and relevant products from the intelligence community, and gathered information from publicly available sources, including reports from civil society and the media. While the USG is not necessarily in a position independently to verify all information received from sources that are viewed as credible based on their history of reporting and their level of access to relevant facts, and the State and Defense Departments have not both been able to validate every item, such information is included in this report where relevant to reported incidents. Within the State and Defense Departments, relevant bureaus with regional, subject matter, technical, and legal expertise provided their input and contributed to the drafting of this report.

While certain events and information in individual country reports below may fall outside of the scope of the NSM-20 reporting requirements – either by happening beyond the period in question or not involving the use of covered defense articles – they are included to provide important context that could be relevant to credibility and reliability assessments for partner government assurances.

NSM-20 Challenges

This first report under NSM-20 highlights the robust and significant security relationships with seven partners who are in active conflict. Nevertheless, this section discusses the various challenges that the USG faced when developing this report. In the context of active conflict, it is challenging to collect accurate and reliable information. USG personnel are often constrained from accessing a conflict zone. This means much of the information for reports like this one are collected from the partner nation, USG contractors, or other third parties, including from other international partners. Collecting this information firsthand is exceedingly difficult. We appreciate deeply the work of journalists, NGOs, humanitarian workers, and other entities and organizations, especially those operating on the ground, who have provided information relevant to this report and that we have considered in preparing it. While reports received from civil society or published in the media often do not, on their own, contain sufficient information to reach firm conclusions about compliance or lack thereof with particular standards, the Departments of State and of Defense also have sought, as part of our analysis, to consider all available and relevant information, including tools and information that are not available to outside organizations, such as operational planning data, intelligence data, and sensitive diplomatic data.

Reliably assessing a partner's conduct can depend on information that is only available to the partner. External actors generally do not have the ability to question relevant, oftentimes junior military personnel at the unit level or access classified military information. External actors also generally do not have the ability to question the military commanders or decisionmakers in the process for particular military operations. A similar point can be made with regard to reports of civilian harm. Reliably assessing what specific practices were applied in a particular incident can require information that was available only to the force that conducted the operation.

In assessing partner government assurances regarding humanitarian assistance, it is important to note that NSM-20 specifies that partner governments must provide an assurance that, consistent with international law, they will not arbitrarily deny, restrict, or otherwise impede U.S. humanitarian assistance efforts. Instances where aid may, in certain circumstances and consistent with international law, be denied, restricted or otherwise impeded, but not necessarily in an arbitrary manner, could include appropriate requirements for dual-use products that can be diverted to military purposes, requirements for humanitarian movements in active combat zones, or other legitimate measures.

Our assessments remain ongoing. We will continually monitor new and relevant information received from parts of the USG, NGOs, and other entities and organizations. We will review existing assessments if they are called into question by new, relevant, credible information that becomes available.

Finally, the short timeline to collect and review data from more than a year created challenges for drafters, particularly given competing demands on a limited number of personnel. No additional resources were available to offices required to implement NSM-20. We will work with Congress to address these resource constraints.

U.S. Conventional Arms Transfer (CAT) Policy

The President's February 2023 CAT policy takes a holistic approach to arms transfer decisions that considers a number of U.S. national security interests, including human rights, security sector governance, and strategic competition. There is a prohibition under the CAT Policy on any arms transfer where the USG assesses "it is more likely than not" that the arms to be transferred would be used in, facilitate, or aggravate the risk of commission of certain serious violations of human rights law or IHL. This policy applies to decisions on whether to authorize the transfer of United States arms to a foreign user, including certain items on the Commerce Control List, the transfer of defense articles, related technical data, and defense services, regardless of the authority or USG department or agency under which the transfer would occur or be authorized.

Civilian Harm Mitigation and Response (CHMR)

The Secretary of Defense has stated that protecting civilians is not only a moral imperative but a strategic priority to achieve mission success. In August 2022, the Secretary of Defense approved the Civilian Harm Mitigation and Response Action Plan (CHMR-AP), which sets forth a series of actions that DoD is taking to improve its approach to CHMR. DoD Instruction (DoDI) 3000.17 dated December 21, 2023, "Civilian Harm Mitigation and Response," sets in place standards to incorporate CHMR into U.S. military operations. Ultimately, CHMR efforts reflect U.S. and professional military values, in particular the importance of protecting and respecting human life and treating civilians with dignity and respect.

DoD is actively developing procedures for integrating CHMR considerations into DoD security cooperation programs and activities, including, among other things, responding to reports of civilian harm by ally or partner forces receiving security cooperation assistance under authorities in chapter 16 of Title 10, U.S. Code. Implementation of CHMR-AP and the DoDI across DoD is ongoing. DoD continues efforts to hire dozens of CHMR subject matter experts, and the referenced development of procedures coordination before final approval.

State Department Civilian Harm Incident Response Guidance (CHIRG)

The protection of civilians in the context of military operations by foreign governments has long been viewed by the State Department as a priority fundamental to advancing both U.S. interests and values. It is also critical to strengthening our relationships with allies and partners. The State Department initiated development of the CHIRG in response to Government Accountability Office recommendations regarding the U.S. response to reports of civilian harm in

Yemen. The State Department recognized the potential use of U.S. munitions in incidents involving civilian harm should be addressed through a globally focused process. The CHIRG, launched in September 2023, establishes a bottom up, institutional process to assess and respond to new incidents of civilian harm in which U.S.-provided defense articles may have been used, take steps to help prevent them from recurring, and to drive partners to ensure military operations are conducted in accordance with international law.

Leahy Laws

The Leahy laws refer to statutory provisions that restrict certain assistance to units of foreign security forces if the Secretary of State or Defense has credible information that the unit committed a gross violations of human rights (GVHR). In this context, GVHRs include torture, extrajudicial killing, enforced disappearance, and rape under the color of law. Allegations of GVHRs by foreign security forces are examined on a fact-specific basis. Where U.S. assistance to a foreign security force is provided in a manner in which the recipient unit or units cannot be identified prior to the transfer of assistance, the law requires the State Department to complete an agreement with the recipient government that it will not provide such assistance to any unit the Department identifies as ineligible under the Leahy law. In addition, the State Department has a process to proactively review allegations of GVHRs.

Human Rights and Rule of Law Training

All equipment transfers under DoD authorities such as 10 U.S.C. 333 (Train and Equip) require human rights and rule of law training for partner nations. The training is specific to the lethality of weapons or systems the partner is receiving, and in general, the more lethal the system or capability, the longer and more in-depth the training required.

The Defense Institute of International Legal Studies (DIILS) is the lead DoD security cooperation resource for rule of law capacity-building with international defense sector officials. DIILS conducts resident courses and mobile programs in support of security cooperation programs under authorities in Title 10, U.S. Code, such as Institutional Capacity Building.

During the period of January 1, 2023 to March 24, 2024, forces from Colombia, Iraq, Kenya, Nigeria, Somalia, and Ukraine received a range of DIILS training.

Through professional and technical courses and specialized instruction, the International Military Education and Training (IMET) program provides students from allied and partner nations valuable training and education on U.S. military practices and standards, including exposure to democratic values and respect for internationally recognized standards of human rights.

End Use Monitoring (EUM)

The objective of the EUM program is to provide a factual basis for the USG to conclude reasonably that a foreign partner is meeting its end use requirements. DoD implements EUM for Foreign Military Sales while the State Department implements EUM for Direct Commercial Sales. DoD's EUM program, Golden Sentry, has the objective to ensure compliance with technology control requirements in order to minimize security risks to the United States, partner nations, and allies. The State Department's EUM program, Blue Lantern, promotes understanding of U.S. defense trade controls by foreign partners, builds mutual confidence with partner governments and industry in the defense trade relationship and supply chains; and mitigates the risk of unauthorized diversion and use of U.S. defense articles. EUM includes follow-on actions to prevent misuse or unauthorized transfer of defense articles or services from title transfer until disposal. The type of defense article or service generally determines the level of monitoring required. USG EUM can include scheduled inspections, physical inventories, and reviews of accountability records.

State Department Human Rights Report

The Country Reports on Human Rights Practices, commonly known as the Human Rights Report (HRR), is an annual report mandated by Congress beginning in 1977. Public servants in U.S. missions abroad and in Washington examine, track, and document the state of human rights in nearly 200 countries and territories around the world. In compiling the annual reports, the State Department draws from a variety of credible, fact-based sources, including reporting from government agencies, NGOs, and media. The HRR helps connect U.S. diplomatic and foreign assistance efforts to the fundamental American value of protecting and promoting respect for universal human rights, while helping to inform the work of civil society, human rights defenders, scholars, multilateral institutions, and others. DoD has not independently reviewed or assessed the information drawn from the 2023 HRR included in this report.

COUNTRY REPORTS

Colombia

Assessment of credible reports or allegations that certain defense articles and, as appropriate, defense services, have been used in a manner not consistent with international law, including international humanitarian law; such assessment shall include any determinations, if they can reasonably be made, as to whether use has occurred in a manner not consistent with international law, and if so, whether the recipient country has pursued appropriate accountability; and a description of the procedures used to make the assessments:

The Colombian government has made significant strides to professionalize its military and ensure it upholds IHL and human rights. The Ministry of Defense issued its first human rights policy in 2008, which mandated that the Ministry, General Staff, and all military services have human rights offices in each unit down to the battalion level. Furthermore, human rights training is universal and adapted according to the level of responsibility, and units are assigned operational lawyers trained on human rights. The Colombian military leadership consistently voice their commitment to respect human rights and the rule of law with an emphasis on zero tolerance for violations of human rights and on human rights as the center of gravity for their institution. Colombian officers have supported human rights-related engagements throughout Latin America and the Caribbean and imparted their training to partner nation's militaries in the Dominican Republic, El Salvador Guatemala, Honduras, Paraguay, and Peru.

The Colombian military has used the U.S.-Colombia Action Plan to provide training to partner nations across Latin America and the Caribbean. The Colombian Ministry of Defense and military have also hosted events to share best practices and lessons learned from their human rights program. Minister of Defense Velasquez has significant legal experience as a judge in combatting corruption and investigating human rights violations and abuses, and, he has committed to prioritizing respect for human rights within the Colombian armed forces.

Assessment and analysis of (1) any credible reports indicating that the use of such defense articles has been found to be inconsistent with established best practices for mitigating civilian harm, and (2) the extent to which efforts to induce effective implementation of such civilian harm mitigation best practices have been incorporated into the relevant United States security assistance program; and a description of the procedures used to make the assessments:

The United States incorporates human rights and respect for law training across a broad spectrum of training and engagements with Colombian partners. Human rights training is conducted at the tactical, operational, and strategic levels, for both State Department and DoD-funded programs with Colombia. Any individual or unit that has been credibly alleged to have been involved in a gross violation of human rights is prevented from receiving USG-funded assistance. Additionally, other kinds of derogatory information can prevent individuals or units from receiving assistance, including information related to the misuse of U.S.-supplied materials. For the vetting process to commence, USG personnel provide detailed information about the unit and its members. For material assistance, this includes providing information on both the individual and unit signing the contracting or procurement documents for the equipment, as well as all units that will be the end-users of the equipment. Vetting must be completed prior to the commencement of the proposed assistance.

In addition, Colombia has undertaken a variety of efforts to implement its obligations under IHL. Colombia has implemented regulations on the use of force by the military and issued a manual on operational law in 2009. Colombia has also taken other steps to disseminate information regarding IHL, including in military training. Further, since 2002, Colombia has employed military lawyers as legal advisers during operations and is considered a regional leader in integration of legal advisers into military operations. Colombia's military justice system is used to ensure accountability for violations committed by members of its armed forces, although this system is in the process of transitioning from an investigatory system to an accusatory system.

Colombia also has an Office of Inspector General (OIG) that routinely inspects and oversees military units and their activity, including efforts that support compliance with IHL. In addition, the Colombian military has taken steps to mitigate harm to non-combatants and is working closely with the U.S. Agency for International

Development (USAID) and other USG entities to reestablish state control in various conflict areas through a phased approach that combines security, counter-narcotics, and socioeconomic development. The Colombian military's presence and operations in these areas have aided in the provision of U.S. and other humanitarian assistance.

Description of any known occurrences of such defense articles not being received by the recipient foreign government that is the intended recipient, or being misused for purposes inconsistent with the intended purposes, and a description of any remedies undertaken:

The USG is not aware of defense articles covered under NSM-20 not being received by the intended foreign government recipient and/or being misused for purposes inconsistent with the intended purposes.

Assessment and analysis of whether each foreign government recipient has abided by the assurances received pursuant to section 1(a)(ii) of the NSM; is in compliance with section 620I of the Foreign Assistance Act of 1961, and whether such recipient has fully cooperated with United States Government efforts and United States Government-supported international efforts to provide humanitarian assistance in an area of armed conflict where the recipient country is using such defense articles and, as appropriate, defense services:

Colombia has fully cooperated with United States Government efforts and United States Government-supported international efforts to provide humanitarian assistance in an area of armed conflict where the recipient country is using covered defense articles.

Iraq

Assessment of credible reports or allegations that certain defense articles and, as appropriate, defense services, have been used in a manner not consistent with international law, including international humanitarian law; such assessment shall include any determinations, if they can reasonably be made, as to whether use has occurred in a manner not consistent with international law, and if so, whether the recipient country has pursued appropriate accountability; and a description of the procedures used to make the assessments:

Although there is ongoing concern over human rights abuses, potential IHL violations, and periodic obstructions of humanitarian access by some elements of the Iraqi security forces (ISF), particularly the Iran-aligned Popular Mobilization Forces (PMF), the United States does not provide covered defense articles or defense services to those entities.

During the reporting period, there were credible reports of potential IHRL violations by government security forces and government-supported armed groups. The State Department's 2023 Country Reports on Human Rights Practices document credible reports of arbitrary or unlawful killings, including extrajudicial killings, as well as torture or other cruel, inhuman, or degrading treatment by government security forces or government-affiliated armed groups.

Nongovernmental organizations also reported disappearances, with the International Committee of the Red Cross receiving nearly 1,000 tracing requests for missing persons from January to July 2023. Additionally, there were credible reports that Iraqi officials employed torture and other cruel, inhuman, or degrading treatment or punishment in jails, detention facilities, and prisons during the reporting period. NGOs indicated that government security forces and government-affiliated forces, including the federal police, the PMF, and units within the internal security services operated with impunity and Iraq maintained very limited accountability for reported violations.

All identified recipients of U.S. foreign assistance undergo vetting to ensure they are not members of foreign terrorist organizations (FTO), sanctioned individuals, nor human rights violators. Material provided to Iraqi security forces undergoes regular end use monitoring and verification.

Through U.S.-led trainings, Iraqi security forces currently receiving covered U.S. defense articles and services have demonstrated an understanding of how professional security forces should operate in active conflict environments, including in compliance with IHL and other international law. U.S.-funded courses for Iraq's security forces over two decades have included and continue to include training on human rights and reducing civilian harm. Since 2003, the United States has provided International Military Education and Training (IMET) funds to support training of Iraqi forces, including through components that train on human rights, respect for the rule of law, and humanitarian assistance response. Additionally, recipients of training provided from the Department of Defense's authority to build capacity (10 U.S.C. 333) are required to take courses on IHL consistent with parameters outlined in NSM-20.

Furthermore, ongoing U.S. Mission Iraq (USMI) visits to Iraq's Counterterrorism Service (CTS) and other Ministry of Interior (MoI) security organizations, including as recently as March 2024, highlighted each organization's ongoing emphasis on human rights training, including through human rights coursework in CTS and MoI training modules. These entities prominently displayed human rights procedures in public spaces, and CTS incorporated them into intake and interview procedures at its facilities. U.S. advisors provide input into coursework on the laws of armed conflict (LOAC) and international human rights law (IHRL) conducted by CTS and attended by MoD participants. Given the close security partnership between Iraq and the United States, U.S. Mission Iraq personnel conduct stringent end use monitoring of defense articles.

Assessment and analysis of (1) any credible reports indicating that the use of such defense articles has been found to be inconsistent with established best practices for mitigating civilian harm, and (2) the extent to which efforts to induce effective implementation of such civilian harm mitigation best practices have been incorporated into the relevant United States security assistance program; and a description of the procedures used to make the assessments:

Iraq and the United States have a highly interconnected defense relationship. Combined Joint Task Force – Operation INHERENT RESOLVE (CJTF-OIR) currently maintains approximately 2,000 Coalition personnel in Iraq, who work daily in an "advise, assist, and enable" capacity with the ISF. U.S. Central Command

(USCENTCOM) hosts biweekly meetings with the ISF. Since February 2024, USCENTCOM has also engaged senior ISF leadership as part of the ongoing Higher Military Commission (HMC) dialogue. These frequent touchpoints provide opportunities for the United States to engage with the ISF regarding the ISF's application of IHL.

Additionally, the Office of Security Cooperation—Iraq (OSC-I) and Defense Attaché teams engage near-daily with the ISF. In all defense transfers, OSC-I works closely with the Government of Iraq. Additionally, the OSC-I Northern Affairs element works consistently with the Iraqi Kurdistan Regional Government (KRG) to continue reform and modernization efforts with the Peshmerga forces, as stated in the DoD-KRG 2022 Memorandum of Understanding.

The Government of Iraq understands that noncompliance with said requirements would jeopardize the significant levels of existing and future USG-funded defense articles afforded to the ISF. At this moment, Iraq is working closely with the United States to normalize and strengthen the bilateral defense relationship.

DoD assesses that the Government of Iraq has been a transparent and cooperative partner in OIR, providing timely reportable information for annual and quarterly accountability as well as congressional reports. The ISF, the primary recipients and users of lethal aid, have been trained by and worked with U.S. and Coalition military forces for more than a decade and have demonstrated an understanding of IHL.

The bilateral U.S.-Iraq security relationship entails continued efforts to work with the ISF, including the Peshmerga, to ensure the enduring defeat of ISIS, while also serving as a key logistical hub for repatriations of displaced persons and foreign terrorist fighters from camps in Syria.

As recently as March 2024, USMI personnel regularly visit Iraqi recipients of covered defense articles, including the CTS, and MoI. These visits serve as opportunities to evaluate each organization's ongoing use of human rights training, including through human rights coursework. USMI has observed that these organizations prominently display information on human rights procedures in public spaces, and CTS incorporates such materials into intake and interview procedures at its facilities. U.S. advisors also provide input into coursework on LOAC and IHRL.

Description of any known occurrences of such defense articles not being received by the recipient foreign government that is the intended recipient, or being misused for purposes inconsistent with the intended purposes, and a description of any remedies undertaken:

The USG is not aware of defense articles covered under NSM-20 not being received by the intended foreign government recipient and/or being misused for purposes inconsistent with the intended purposes.

Assessment and analysis of whether each foreign government recipient is in compliance with section 620I of the Foreign Assistance Act of 1961, and whether such recipient has fully cooperated with United States Government efforts and United States Government-supported international efforts to provide humanitarian assistance in an area of armed conflict where the recipient country is using such defense articles and, as appropriate, defense services:

The Government of Iraq relies significantly on assistance from the United States and other donor partners and has not arbitrarily impeded or restricted U.S. humanitarian assistance in areas of current active armed conflict. The Government of Iraq remains highly cognizant of the close scrutiny of usage of defense articles it receives from the United States and recognizes the challenges it will face if reporting implicates the Government of Iraq's usage in potential violations of IHL or if the Government of Iraq impedes the delivery of humanitarian assistance. ISF that are recipients of U.S. security assistance have not impeded humanitarian assistance and have been compliant with international law. Although some units of the ISF, including the PMF, have occasionally obstructed humanitarian access or committed human rights violations, we do not provide support to those entities. Moreover, in June 2023, the UN Secretary-General stated in a public report that the UN recognized and welcomed the Government of Iraq's concerted effort toward the decrease in verified humanitarian access restrictions, in particular by the ISF.

While USG humanitarian partners do occasionally experience obstacles in the delivery of humanitarian assistance, we assess that impediments are neither systemic nor widespread. By and large, the Government of Iraq remains willing to engage with the USG, other donors, and humanitarian actors on humanitarian concerns, even if its capacity and will to change course when needed are inconsistent. The general population's access to humanitarian assistance is highly constrained across Iraq for a variety of reasons, but access by humanitarian organizations has improved since January 2023 given increased security and reduced movement restrictions for people and goods.

Israel

On October 7, 2023, Hamas, Palestinian Islamic Jihad, and other Palestinian terrorists launched an unprovoked, large-scale attack on Israel from the Gaza Strip, killing an estimated 1,200 individuals, injuring more than 5,400, intentionally targeting civilians without any military justification, and abducting 253 hostages, including American citizens. There are also credible reports that individuals associated with these organizations raped or committed other acts of sexual violence against women and girls killed and abducted on October 7. Hamas had previously launched attacks against Israel from Gaza, including in 2008, 2012, 2014, and 2021. Further, Hamas does not follow any portion of and consistently violates IHL.

Israel has conducted a sustained military operation in Gaza in response to the October 7 attacks and hostage-taking, with the stated objectives of destroying Hamas's military capabilities and dismantling its infrastructure. The conflict has resulted in the deaths of an estimated 34,700 Palestinians and injured more than 78,200 in this reporting period, a significant percentage of whom are reported to be women and children. The Hamas-controlled Gaza Ministry of Health is the primary source for these numbers, which international organizations generally deem credible, but do not differentiate between Hamas fighters and civilians. The Government of Israel has asserted that approximately half of the 34,700 killed in Gaza have been Hamas fighters, though we do not have the ability to verify this estimate. The conflict has displaced the vast majority of Palestinians in Gaza and resulted in a severe humanitarian crisis.

Israel has had to confront an extraordinary military challenge: Hamas has embedded itself deliberately within and underneath the civilian population to use civilians as human shields. Hamas intentionally uses schools, hospitals, residential buildings, and international organization facilities for military purposes. It has constructed a vast tunnel network beneath this civilian infrastructure not to protect civilians, but to hide its leaders and fighters and from which it stages and launches attacks. Hamas has not expressed regret for the intentional targeting of Israeli civilians, and its charter and statements by its leadership continue to call for the destruction of Israel. Hamas continues to hold more than 100 hostages, continues to fire rockets into Israel indiscriminately, and has pledged to conduct attacks on the scale of October 7th again. Military experts describe Gaza as being as difficult a battlespace as any military has faced in modern warfare.

The United States has supported Israel's right to defend itself in the wake of October 7, both from the continuing threat it faces from Hamas and in the broader region, and the United States is committed by law and policy to Israel maintaining its Qualitative Military Edge. The covered defense articles we have provided during this period have helped Israel maintain deterrence against Iran, Hezbollah, and other Iranian-backed proxies in the region, advancing our objective of preventing the conflict from spreading. We have also made clear the imperatives as Israel defends itself of adhering to IHL, protecting humanitarian workers, facilitating the flow of humanitarian assistance, and minimizing civilian casualties.

Throughout this period, the USG has engaged at all levels with the Government of Israel to understand Israel's view of the applicable legal frameworks relevant to the ongoing Israel-Hamas conflict, as well as to further our understanding of the procedures and mechanisms upon which Israel relies to integrate IHL compliance into their approach to combat operations, civilian protection, and humanitarian assistance. In the course of those discussions, Government of Israel officials confirmed their commitment to ongoing dialogue on IHL issues, including as related to the NSM-20 assurances and any incidents of concern.

Israel has institutions and processes charged with upholding the implementation of IHL. Israeli military lawyers can and do give binding legal advice during military operations, and the Israeli Supreme Court may provide judicial review of past targeting and/or operational decisions made during armed conflict. Prior to the conflict in Gaza, the IDF sent an average of approximately 500 personnel to the United States annually for relevant DoD-sponsored training. In many of these courses, IDF personnel are trained to U.S. standards on civilian harm mitigation.

In the course of U.S. engagements during this period, the Government of Israel has identified a number of processes for ensuring compliance with IHL that are embedded at all levels of their military decision-making. The Government of Israel has provided written analysis of its legal positions related to its military operations and described in detail its procedures for integrating legal review into targeting decisions and other aspects of military operations. It has also identified several domestic accountability mechanisms aimed at investigating and remediating violations of its rules of engagement and IHL. The current Military Advocate General has stated publicly that she is investigating incidents in which Israel Defense Forces (IDF) soldiers are alleged to have acted in contravention to IDF protocols and IHL. Israel also appointed a retired Major General and former head of the IDF J3 to lead investigations into incidents in Gaza involving the IDF under the IDF's independent, fact-finding assessment mechanism (FFAM). To date, Israel has confirmed that it has opened a number of criminal investigations, which are ongoing, including into allegations related to deaths and treatment of detainees and allegations of violations of IHL. The FFAM also continues to examine hundreds of incidents to consider possible misconduct in the context of ongoing military operations. Recognizing such investigations and legal processes take time, to date the USG is unaware of any Israeli prosecutions for violations of IHL or civilian harm since October 7.

Israel has, upon request, shared some information on specific incidents implicating IHL, some details of its targeting choices, and some battle damage assessments. Although we have gained insight into Israel's procedures and rules, we do not have complete information on how these processes are implemented. Israel has not shared complete information to verify whether U.S. defense articles covered under NSM-20 were specifically used in actions that have been alleged as violations of IHL or IHRL in Gaza, or in the West Bank and East Jerusalem during the period of the report. Limited information has been shared to date in response to USG inquiries regarding incidents under review to determine whether U.S. munitions were used in incidents involving civilian harm. However, certain Israeli-operated systems are entirely U.S.-origin (e.g., crewed attack aircraft) and are likely to have been involved in incidents that raise concerns about Israel's IHL compliance.

Assessment of credible reports or allegations that certain defense articles and, as appropriate, defense services, have been used in a manner not consistent with international law, including international humanitarian law; such assessment shall include any determinations, if they can reasonably be made, as to whether use has occurred in a manner not consistent with international law, and if so, whether the recipient country has pursued appropriate accountability; and a description of the procedures used to make the assessments:

As reflected in the 2016 Memorandum of Understanding with Israel and pursuant to annual U.S. appropriations acts, the United States provides significant security assistance, including defense articles and services, to Israel on an annual basis. This support will be augmented by supplemental appropriations since October 7. In any conflict involving foreign partners, it is often difficult to make swift, definitive assessments or determinations on whether specific U.S. defense articles or services have been used in a manner not consistent with international law. The nature of the conflict in Gaza and the compressed review period in this initial report amplify those challenges.

However, there have been sufficient reported incidents to raise serious concerns. As described more fully below, the State Department has received reporting from multiple credible UN and non-governmental sources on alleged human rights violations by Israeli forces during the reporting period. The State Department's 2023 Country Reports on Human Rights Practices document credible reports of alleged human rights abuses by Israeli security forces, including arbitrary or unlawful killings, enforced disappearance, torture, and serious abuses in conflict. Credible UN, NGO, and media sources have reported that since October 7, Israeli security forces have arrested large numbers of Palestinians suspected of being Hamas militants and transported them from Gaza to Israel, where some were allegedly abused during their detentions. NGOs have disputed claims that all of these detainees are Hamas militants. There are also allegations of Israeli security forces using excessive force against Palestinians in the West Bank and East Jerusalem in the course of counterterrorism operations. The UN reported that 2023 was the deadliest year on record in the West Bank prior to October 7, and there was a significant intensification of killings and other incidents of violence in the West Bank in the following months. Palestinians killed in operations by Israeli security forces included both militants and civilians while Israeli civilians were also killed by Palestinian terrorists during this period. Extremist settlers have been responsible for acts of violence and intimidation against Palestinians in the West Bank, including incidents where Israeli security forces may have played an abetting role or failed to effectively intervene.

Israeli officials have stated that Israel complies with IHL and continues to strengthen efforts to minimize civilian harm. Given the nature of the conflict in Gaza, with Hamas seeking to hide behind civilian populations and infrastructure and expose them to Israeli military action, as well as the lack of USG personnel on the ground in Gaza, it is difficult to assess or reach conclusive findings on individual incidents. Nevertheless, given Israel's significant reliance on U.S.-made defense articles, it is reasonable to assess that defense articles covered under NSM-20 have been used by Israeli security forces since October 7 in instances inconsistent with its IHL obligations or with established best practices for mitigating civilian harm. Israel's own concern about such incidents is reflected in the fact it has a number of internal investigations underway. At the same time, it is also important to emphasize that a country's overall commitment to IHL is not necessarily disproven by individual IHL violations, so long as that country is taking appropriate steps to investigate and where appropriate determine accountability for IHL violations. As this report notes, Israel does have a number of ongoing, active criminal investigations pending and there are hundreds of cases under administrative review.

The U.S. Intelligence Community (IC) notes that security forces in Israel, which is involved in an active war against Hamas, have inflicted harm on civilians in military or security operations, potentially using U.S.-provided equipment. The IC has no direct indication of Israel intentionally targeting civilians. The IC assesses that Israel could do more to avoid civilian harm, however.

One specific area of concern is the impact of Israel's military operations on humanitarian actors. Despite regular engagement from humanitarian actors and repeated USG interventions with Israeli officials on deconfliction/coordination procedures, the IDF has struck humanitarian workers and facilities. While Israel repeatedly committed to improve deconfliction and implemented some additional measures, those changes did not fully prevent subsequent strikes involving humanitarian workers and facilities during the reporting period. The USG will continue to press the Government of Israel on the need to do more to create a permissive and safe environment for delivery and distribution of aid.

The UN reports that more than 250 humanitarian workers have been killed in the course of their work or in other circumstances. Multiple military operations have taken place in protected or de-conflicted sites or in areas designated for evacuees. Some of these incidents during the reporting period that have received widespread attention in media or are cited by humanitarian organizations as illustrative of the operating environment in Gaza are noted below. As noted above, we are not able to reach definitive conclusions on whether defense articles covered by NSM-20 were used in these or other individual strikes.

- 4/9/2024: Small arms fire reportedly struck a UN International Children's Emergency Fund vehicle and World Food Program fuel truck in a convoy south of the Salahedin checkpoint. UN staff reported IDF patrols were the source of fire. Israeli authorities denied responsibility. The [UN] submitted a formal complaint to the Coordinator of Government Activities in the Territories (COGAT).

- 4/1/2024: Seven World Central Kitchen (WCK) workers, including an American citizen, were killed by three successive IDF strikes on their aid convoy despite WCK having coordinated with the IDF; Israel accepted responsibility and conducted an immediate investigation, called the incident a "grave mistake," said the IDF misidentified the vehicles, dismissed four officers responsible, formally reprimanded relevant commanders, and said prosecutions are being considered.

- 2/29/2024: At least 118 people reportedly were killed and approximately 760 people were injured along the coastal road southwest of Gaza City when crowds gathered around trucks carrying humanitarian aid. An IDF command review of the incident reported that IDF troops fired at individuals who approached their forces at the IDF checkpoint adjacent to the end of the lengthy convoy. The IDF initially fired warning shots, but subsequently fired at individuals' lower extremities when the group continued to approach. While the GOI acknowledged IDF shooting-related fatalities might have ensued, it asserted that most civilian deaths occurred due to stampeding and trucks driving over people. Accounts from NGO and media reporting dispute this assertion. The IDF General Staff's FFAM continues to investigate the incident.

- 2/20/2024: IDF tank fire reportedly killed two people and injured six others – five of whom were women or children – in a Medecins Sans Frontieres (MSF) guesthouse in Khan Younis Governorate's Al Mawasi area, according to MSF. MSF reports Israeli forces had been clearly informed of the precise location of the guesthouse, and the site clearly displayed humanitarian identification.

- 1/18/2024: An Israeli airstrike reportedly hit a residential site used by humanitarian staff from the International Rescue Committee (IRC) and Medical Aid for Palestinians UK (MAP), injuring two staff members and damaging the building beyond repair. IRC and MAP indicated that the site had been deconflicted with the IDF, and that Israel provided varied responses to IRC and MAP inquiries about the strike. As a result, IRC and MAP surgeons suspended medical work at Nasser Hospital.

Additionally, there are numerous credible UN, NGO, and media reports of Israeli airstrikes impacting civilians and civilian objects unrelated to humanitarian operations that have raised questions about Israel's compliance with its legal obligations under IHL and with best practices for mitigating civilian harm. These include reported incidents involving strikes on civilian infrastructure and other sites protected from being made the object of attack absent use for a military purpose; certain strikes in densely populated areas; strikes taken under circumstances that call into question whether expected civilian harm may have been excessive relative to the reported military objective; or failure to provide effective warning or take appropriate precautions to protect civilians. Strikes on protected sites do not necessarily constitute violations of IHL, as such sites can be legitimate targets if used for military purposes. However, all military operations must always comply with IHL rules, including distinction, proportionality, and precautions. Because Hamas uses civilian infrastructure for military purposes and civilians as human shields, it is often difficult to determine facts on the ground in an active war zone of this nature and the presence of legitimate military targets across Gaza. As noted above, the reported death tolls in Gaza generally do not differentiate between Hamas and civilian deaths, further complicating efforts to precisely assess the civilian impact. Several examples of these strikes during the reporting period include:

- 3/8/2024: An Israeli airstrike reportedly killed dozens sheltering in Deir al-Balah, including an Anera humanitarian worker. Anera reported it had shared the coordinates of the site with COGAT. Anera has raised concerns about the lack of effective deconfliction in Gaza and called for an independent investigation.

- 12/24/2023: Israeli airstrikes on a home in the Maghazi refugee camp, reportedly killing 90 with an unknown number additionally injured. Israel indicated that it was investigating the incident.

- 10/31/2023 and 11/1/2023: Israeli airstrikes on the Jabailia refugee camp, reportedly killing dozens of civilians, including several dozen children, injuring hundreds more, and significantly damaging civilian infrastructure. The IDF reported these airstrikes successfully targeted a senior Hamas commander and underground Hamas facilities. Israel said the munitions used in the strike led to the collapse of tunnels and the buildings and infrastructure above them as well as significant reported civilian harm in a densely populated area.

- 10/22/2023: An Israeli airstrike on a civilian home in Deir al-Balah, reportedly killing 18 civilians including 12 children. Amnesty International identified U.S.-origin munition fragments at the site but this has not been confirmed.

  10/9/2023: Israeli airstrikes on a marketplace in Jabaliya refugee camp, reportedly killing dozens, including many Hamas fighters according to the IDF. Israel reported these strikes sought to destroy a significant Hamas tunnel complex.

Assessment and analysis of (1) any credible reports indicating that the use of such defense articles has been found to be inconsistent with established best practices for mitigating civilian harm, and (2) the extent to which efforts to induce effective implementation of such civilian harm mitigation best practices have been incorporated into the relevant United States security assistance program; and a description of the procedures used to make the assessments:

The USG reviewed numerous reports of civilian harm resulting from IDF operations during the reporting period, which raised serious questions with respect to whether Israel was upholding established best practices for mitigating civilian harm.

Israel has provided hundreds of tactical pauses to allow civilians to leave combat zones. These range from an evacuation order at the beginning of the war for civilians in northern Gaza to move to the south two weeks before ground operations began; to establishing daily four-hour humanitarian pauses, with three hours notice, and evacuation corridors to allow for north-south movements; to hundreds of smaller-scale pauses in specific neighborhoods to allow civilians to procure supplies and/or seek medical care. The IDF used numerous methods to inform citizens of these pauses, including dropping leaflets, making automated phone calls, and sending SMS text messages. Israel has a sophisticated system for identifying where civilians are located in order to try to minimize civilian harm. However, UN and humanitarian organizations have reported Israeli civilian harm mitigation efforts as inconsistent, ineffective, and inadequate, failing to provide protection to vulnerable civilians who cannot or chose not to relocate, including persons with disabilities, persons receiving medical treatment, children, and the infirm. Humanitarian organizations reported further that phone/SMS messages were ineffective during IDF-generated telecommunications blackouts, and civilians received insufficient notice, inaccurate or vague information on where people should go, and on safe evacuation routes. Many of the IDF-designated areas to which civilians were directed to seek safety lacked adequate shelter, water, sanitation, food, medical care, security or other support. The reported rate of civilian harm in the conflict also raises serious questions about the efficacy of Israeli precautionary measures, notwithstanding Hamas' deliberate embedding within and use of civilian and humanitarian infrastructure as shelter.

The IDF coordinated with foreign governments and NGOs to create no-strike lists of facilities operated by foreign governments, NGOs, and international organizations. However, since the beginning of the conflict in Gaza, the UN has reported 169 of its facilities in Gaza have been destroyed or damaged. These make up just a fraction of the sites characterized by the USG as Category I protected sites that are given heightened protection under targeting procedures, including diplomatic, medical, education, religious/cultural, and other facilities. Numerous incidents have been reported in which civilians have been hit at these sites. Many of these incidents reportedly have been the result of Hamas launching attacks on Israeli troops from these protected facilities or safe zones, or firing rockets into Israel from them, followed by the IDF returning fire to eliminate the threat. IDF leadership has also cited other occasions where they chose not to engage given the presence of civilians. During this period, 85 alleged incidents of civilian harm involving Israeli military operations in Gaza have been submitted to the CHIRG for evaluation, and approximately 40 percent of those cases have been closed.

Following the WCK incident on April 1, 2024, Israel took initial steps to set up a new Humanitarian Coordination and De-confliction Cell to better ensure the safety of humanitarian providers. Humanitarian organizations have consistently underscored that real-time communication between IDF units and humanitarian workers on the ground, particularly at checkpoints, is imperative to realizing concrete improvement in deconfliction and coordination. Humanitarian organizations repeatedly requested approval from COGAT to bring in equipment necessary to enable this communication, with COGAT raising concerns about potential diversion to Hamas for military purposes. COGAT recently approved this equipment, with deployment in initial stages. We continue to engage with the Government of Israel to encourage it to take necessary steps to improve its deconfliction mechanisms.

The IDF coordinates closely with USCENTCOM, Security Cooperation Office, and Defense Attaché teams in Israel on IHL in addition to frequent engagements on issues related to the conflict at the Secretary or Under Secretary levels. On numerous occasions and at various levels, IDF and Israel Ministry of Defense personnel have shared with U.S. counterparts descriptions of Israel's efforts to implement IHL in their operations in Gaza. IDF officials have shared details about their targeting processes, including an extensive sensitive site list, legal advisors embedded in the target approval process, and investigation protocol for incidents of unanticipated collateral damage. The IDF has also shared images and videos demonstrating real-time capabilities to depict civilian population movement and has shared evidence of certain strikes that were aborted when civilians were observed in the target area. DoD does not observe real-time targeting, however.

The IDF has also created a map dividing Gaza into more than 300 sectors, which has been shared with civilians and humanitarian organizations in Gaza. The IDF develops assessments of the level of civilian presence in each sector of the map, using cell phone data among other sources, while also working to update these assessments as the situation evolves. However, humanitarian organizations have raised serious concerns regarding the efficacy of this system, and the USG continues to engage Israel to improve these methods.

The IDF has undertaken steps to implement IHL obligations for the protection of civilians in the current conflict, including the requirements related to distinction, proportionality, and precautions in offensive operations. As reflected above, however, the USG lacks full visibility into Israel's application of these principles and procedures. In addition, the Government of Israel has asserted it takes steps to mitigate the risk of civilian harm when conducting military operations, such as providing advance warnings, employing specific procedures for determining targets and carrying out attacks, including choice of weapons and munitions, and implementing restrictive measures to protect sites such as hospitals, schools, places of worship and UN facilities. Israel has also asserted that its processes provide opportunities for the IDF to validate the presence or absences of civilians, including through the collection of intelligence that would support real-time assessment of civilian harm, and have led to aborted airstrikes when unexpected civilians have appeared. While Israel has the knowledge, experience, and tools to implement best practices for mitigating civilian harm in its military operations, the results on the ground, including high levels of civilian casualties, raise substantial questions as to whether the IDF is using them effectively in all cases. This includes the WCK strike, in which Israel has acknowledged that IDF operators did not follow applicable rules of engagement, and which led the Israelis to take steps to discipline IDF personnel.

The State Department will continue to engage with the Government of Israel to establish a dedicated channel focused on supporting more timely and fully-informed work by the CHIRG to review incidents of concern and to make recommendations to reduce the risk of civilian harm.

Description of any known occurrences of such defense articles not being received by the recipient foreign government that is the intended recipient, or being misused for purposes inconsistent with the intended purposes, and a description of any remedies undertaken:

The USG is not aware of defense articles covered under NSM-20 not being received by the intended foreign government recipient and/or being misused for purposes inconsistent with the intended purposes.

Assessment and analysis of whether each foreign government recipient is in compliance with section 620I of the Foreign Assistance Act of 1961, and whether

such recipient has fully cooperated with United States Government efforts and United States Government-supported international efforts to provide humanitarian assistance in an area of armed conflict where the recipient country is using such defense articles and, as appropriate, defense services:

Since October 7, the United States has led international efforts to address the humanitarian crisis in Gaza, including providing significant contributions for food, water, medical, and other essential supplies and coordinating delivery mechanisms with Israel, Egypt, Jordan, UN agencies and humanitarian partners. If not for sustained engagement by the United States with the Israeli government at the highest levels, the humanitarian crisis that has persisted for the past several months would have been even more dire.

During the period since October 7, and particularly in the initial months, Israel did not fully cooperate with USG efforts and USG-supported international efforts to maximize humanitarian assistance flow to and distribution within Gaza. There were numerous instances during the period of Israeli actions that delayed or had a negative effect on the delivery of aid to Gaza. Specific examples include:

- Some senior Israeli government officials have been actively involved in encouraging protests against and attacks on aid convoys that delayed their entry into Gaza. Israeli civilian protestors periodically blocked entry points into Gaza during a multi-week period in January and February, resulting in reduced aid flows.

- As noted above, there have been strikes on coordinated humanitarian movements and deconflicted humanitarian sites that created an exceptionally difficult environment for distributing and delivering aid.

- There have been denials or delays of specific movements of humanitarian actors.

- Extensive bureaucratic delays with regard to implementation of political commitments made by Israeli leaders have further slowed the delivery of assistance to civilians in Gaza.

- Inconsistent rejections of humanitarian relief supplies and a lack of standardized processes significantly reduced aid workers' ability to transport humanitarian items into Gaza. In particular, Israel has failed to provide a clear, definitive list of items allowed into or prohibited from entering Gaza because of dual-use concerns. It also has, on occasion, stretched dual-use issues to a concerning degree.

- Humanitarian organizations continue to report a lack of clarity around how cargo is validated at checkpoints along supply routes and there is no standardized practice dictated by COGAT to prevent approved commodities from being rejected at various inspection points.

- Delays in visa issuance for humanitarian staff by Israel's Ministry of Welfare and Social Affairs have exacerbated the shortage of relief personnel and made the delivery of aid into Gaza more difficult. In late April, as a result of transfer of the authority over visa issuance to the Ministry of Foreign Affairs and U.S. intervention, all but a small number of pending visa requests were approved for periods of at least six months.

As noted above, assessments under NSM-20 must also factor in whether requirements applied to efforts to provide humanitarian assistance are arbitrary. Getting aid to Palestinians in Gaza is a complex undertaking in an active war zone. The destruction of civilian infrastructure, the embedding of Hamas in the civilian population, and ongoing military operations by the IDF have complicated aid delivery and exacerbated the humanitarian crisis, as have Israeli concerns about Hamas appropriating dual-use items for military purposes. Hamas has at times sought to direct the distribution of humanitarian assistance not to maximize the benefits to civilians in Gaza but rather to try to maintain its effective control of governance functions.

The USG worked with Government of Israel, international partners, and humanitarian organizations to resolve these and other challenges. Senior members of the Israeli government have also worked to overcome the objections of individual government ministers opposed to Israel having a role in addressing the humanitarian needs of the civilian population in Gaza. After the Hamas attacks on October 7, humanitarian aid began to enter Gaza as of October 21. At USG urging, Israel established the initial humanitarian crossing mechanism at

Rafah, opened Kerem Shalom and Gate 96, allowed flour to move via Ashdod port, enabled fuel deliveries, and cooperated with international efforts to open air and maritime aid corridors. To prevent protestors from disrupting aid movements into Gaza, the Minister of Defense instructed the IDF to declare the crossing points closed military zones and acted more effectively to remove and arrest the protesters, which facilitated an increase in aid to previous levels. However, aid levels remain below what is necessary to meet the nutritional, medical, and sanitary needs of the population. UN agencies and NGOs have assessed that aid deliveries remain below levels necessary to fully mitigate the potential risk of famine, while Israel has consistently disputed famine warnings.

More recently, Israel has substantially increased humanitarian access and aid flow into Gaza, reaching significantly higher levels that require continued upward trajectory to meet immense needs. On April 4, President Biden secured commitment from Prime Minister Netanyahu on a series of concrete steps that – if fully implemented and sustained – would substantially improve the delivery and distribution of assistance and materially improve humanitarian conditions for civilians in Gaza.

In recent weeks, Israel acted on many of these steps, including significantly increasing the number of trucks entering Gaza, opening the Erez crossing, facilitating humanitarian shipments through Ashdod port, expanding the use of the Jordan corridor, and repairing and opening routes to northern Gaza. The volume of aid entering Gaza measurably increased – April showed the highest volume of humanitarian and commercial supplies since the conflict began. The Israeli government reopened and/or repaired the three major water pipelines into Gaza, but there remains damage to the distribution network within Gaza that limits water flow and the overall supply of water remains inadequate to meet the basic human needs of 2.1 million Palestinians. Israel increased the supply of fuel to humanitarian actors, including to newly established bakeries in northern Gaza. Israel must sustain these actions and implement a number of commitments not yet acted upon in order to stabilize humanitarian conditions in Gaza.

While the USG has had deep concerns during the period since October 7 about action and inaction by Israel that contributed significantly to a lack of sustained and predictable delivery of needed assistance at scale, and the overall level reaching Palestinian civilians – while improved – remains insufficient, we do not currently assess that the Israeli government is prohibiting or otherwise restricting the transport or delivery of U.S. humanitarian assistance within the meaning of section 620I of the Foreign Assistance Act. This is an ongoing assessment and we will continue to monitor and respond to any challenges to the delivery of aid to Palestinian civilians in Gaza moving forward.

Kenya

Assessment of credible reports or allegations that certain defense articles and, as appropriate, defense services, have been used in a manner not consistent with international law, including international humanitarian law; such assessment shall include any determinations, if they can reasonably be made, as to whether use has occurred in a manner not consistent with international law, and if so, whether the recipient country has pursued appropriate accountability; and a description of the procedures used to make the assessments:

During the reporting period, there were credible reports of potential IHRL violations by government security forces and government-supported armed groups. The State Department's 2023 Country Reports on Human Rights Practices document credible reports of arbitrary or unlawful killings, including extrajudicial killings as well as the use of torture and violence during interrogations.

Nongovernmental organizations reported Kenyan security forces used excessive force against demonstrators during protests that took place between March and July 2023, including through the use of crowd control items such as teargas as well as firearms with live ammunition. The Kenya National Commission on Human Rights recorded 24 deaths during protests from suffocation and shootings. Additionally, NGOs reported more than 100 extrajudicial killings and over 400 cases of torture between January and September 2023. NGOs indicated Kenyan police forces operated with impunity, as the government neither acknowledged alleged human rights violations nor held individual police officers accountable for their actions and the resulting harm during the protests from March to July 2023.

The Government of Kenya has reaffirmed its commitment to accountability based on the Kenya Defence Forces (KDF) Act of 2012. According to the Act, the KDF shall "train staff to the highest possible standards of competence and integrity and to respect human rights and fundamental freedoms and dignity."

In addition, the government has publicly stated that the Ministry of Defense has opened its doors for complaints both internally and externally under the existing chain of command in accordance with the 2012 act. In September 2023, Cabinet Secretary of Defense Aden Duale hosted the chair of Kenya's Commission for Administrative Justice (CAJ), commonly known as the Office of the Ombudsman, and said that the MoD is open to having a CAJ liaison officer within the Ministry to enable access to information.

In addition, Kenya has undertaken a variety of efforts to implement its obligations under IHL. For example, Kenya has established a national committee on implementation of IHL, convened by the International Law Division of the Kenyan Ministry of Justice.

Kenya also has taken steps to disseminate information regarding IHL, including issuing a military manual on the law of armed conflict, which emphasizes the importance of training. Kenya's national council for law reporting also publishes online a number of IHL treaties, including the 1949 Geneva Convention. Similarly, Kenya employs military lawyers, and Kenya has a system of military justice that can be used to ensure accountability for violations committed by members of its armed forces. There is also information indicating that Kenyan leaders have set a command climate emphasizing the important of compliance with IHL.

Assessment and analysis of (1) any credible reports indicating that the use of such defense articles has been found to be inconsistent with established best practices for mitigating civilian harm, and (2) the extent to which efforts to induce effective implementation of such civilian harm mitigation best practices have been incorporated into the relevant United States security assistance program; and a description of the procedures used to make the assessments:

From International Military Education Training courses in the United States for large annual cadres of KDF to large, joint, multinational exercises hosted in Kenya, Civilian Harm Mitigation and Response is a deliberate narrative and core theme of U.S.-Kenyan military-to-military engagements. The United States has significant security cooperation programs with Kenya, which span multiple lines of effort across numerous military capabilities, including instruction on IHL.

DoD provides specific training to the KDF on Air-to-Ground Integration (AGI), which establishes doctrine, tactics, techniques, and procedures to build capability to plan and execute operations in a manner consistent with IHL and best practices for mitigating civilian harm.

Description of any known occurrences of such defense articles not being received by the recipient foreign government that is the intended recipient, or being misused for purposes inconsistent with the intended purposes, and a description of any remedies undertaken:

The USG is not aware of defense articles covered under NSM-20 not being received by the intended foreign government recipient and/or being misused for purposes inconsistent with the intended purposes.

Assessment and analysis of whether each foreign government recipient is in compliance with section 620I of the Foreign Assistance Act of 1961, and whether such recipient has fully cooperated with United States Government efforts and United States Government-supported international efforts to provide humanitarian assistance in an area of armed conflict where the recipient country is using such defense articles and, as appropriate, defense services:

In the past, allegations have been made of food aid being diverted in Kenya, but these allegations implicate individual politicians rather than the KDF. While USAID and its humanitarian partners can experience occasional obstacles in the delivery of humanitarian assistance, impediments are neither systematic nor widespread. The KDF has been accused of participating in illicit trade of goods, but it has not been reported for restricting humanitarian assistance in international peacekeeping operations.

Nigeria

Assessment of credible reports or allegations that certain defense articles and, as appropriate, defense services, have been used in a manner not consistent with international law, including international humanitarian law; such assessment shall include any determinations, if they can reasonably be made, as to whether use has occurred in a manner not consistent with international law, and if so, whether the recipient country has pursued appropriate accountability; and a description of the procedures used to make the assessments:

Nigeria has undertaken a variety of efforts to implement its obligations under IHL, including related to dissemination of and training on IHL. Although efforts to incorporate Nigerian military lawyers into advice during military operations are nascent, Nigeria has military lawyers and a military justice system, which it has rapidly expanded over the past two years.

At all levels of the USG, officials discuss with Nigerian counterparts ways to reduce incidents of civilian harm and encourage transparency and accountability when such incidents do occur. DoD is working with Nigeria to strengthen and professionalize the Nigerian Armed Forces through development of and adherence to rules-based structures. Through multi-year efforts, DoD is working to strengthen Nigeria's Advanced Infantry and Special Operations Forces and capabilities for intelligence, surveillance, and reconnaissance.

Furthermore, the United States has an ongoing Air-to-Ground Integration initiative with Nigeria, which addresses key capabilities that significantly contribute to civilian harm mitigation. In addition, Nigeria recently purchased a training package through the foreign military sales program to support additional training and capacity-building for civilian harm mitigation over five years. The Defense Security Cooperation University (DSCU)'s Institute for Security Governance will provide this training, which includes education and training supporting increased awareness and compliance with human rights and IHL, throughout the Nigerian Armed Forces.

During the reporting period, there were no credible reports of U.S. defense articles or services used in a manner not consistent with international law. There were credible reports of potential IHL and IHRL violations by military forces not involving U.S.-funded defense articles and services, though investigations and/or court martial proceedings were reportedly conducted. Nigeria classifies most investigations and court martial outcomes making the outcome of its investigations of credible reports unclear.

NGOs reported Nigerian security forces routinely used excessive force in the course of their duties, as well as using physical violence and torture in jails and prisons. Impunity for torture remained a significant problem for Nigerian security forces, including in the police, military, and Department of State Services – Nigeria's primary internal security agency. Nigerian operations against ISIS-West Africa, Boko Haram, and criminal groups also resulted in concerning incidents of civilian harm during the reporting period that raise concerns about potential IHL violations. An illustrative list follows:

- 1/3/2023: The Nigerian Army conducted a drone strike against a religious gathering in Kaduna State that killed at least 85 individuals and possibly as many as 120 persons in what it characterized as a mistaken strike as it targeted terrorists moving in the area. The Nigerian government covered all medical costs for victims and provided other assistance to the victims and community. The USG has raised this incident with Nigerian representatives.

- 1/24/2023: An airstrike reportedly against criminal bandits in the rural community of Kwatiri killed an estimated 39 civilians, predominately herders gathered to retrieve their confiscated cattle. On January 28, 2024, the Nigerian government admitted innocent civilians were killed in the strike and reported that it was working to provide compensation to victims.

- 4/2024: An airstrike in Zamfara state reportedly killed at least 33 persons. The Nigerian Air Force claimed the strike targeted and killed terrorists in the area, but residents reported those killed were civilians, including children.

As detailed further below, the Nigerian military is working to improve and follow civilian harm mitigation best practices with U.S. assistance, and the current government has recently shown a willingness to address these incidents quickly and transparently.

Assessment and analysis of (1) any credible reports indicating that the use of such defense articles has been found to be inconsistent with established best practices for mitigating civilian harm, and (2) the extent to which efforts to induce effective implementation of such civilian harm mitigation best practices have been incorporated into the relevant United States security assistance program; and a description of the procedures used to make the assessments:

There have been no credible reports that covered defense articles have been used by Nigeria's military in a manner inconsistent with established best practices for mitigating civilian harm, including practices that have been adopted by the United States military, and including measures implemented in response to the CHMR-AP or incidents reviewed pursuant to the Department of State's CHIRG during the reporting period.

U.S.-Nigeria security cooperation includes an intensive focus on reducing civilian harm. The Nigerian military is working to improve training and legal advice, and to follow such best practices. State Department and DoD-funded U.S. security assistance programs integrate human rights and civilian harm mitigation training and concepts as key components of the programs. Additionally, in a first of its kind case of a foreign military sale of attack helicopters, Nigeria paid $25 million for an air-to-ground integration program that will help mitigate civilian harm across its three military services. They also have requested to purchase precision weapons specifically to reduce collateral harm. Current and proposed U.S. security assistance programs are designed to complement this program in facilitating the development and implementation of civilian harm mitigation doctrine, policies, and procedures across the armed forces of Nigeria.

Description of any known occurrences of such defense articles not being received by the recipient foreign government that is the intended recipient, or being misused for purposes inconsistent with the intended purposes, and a description of any remedies undertaken:

The USG is not aware of defense articles covered under NSM-20 not being received by the intended foreign government recipient and/or being misused for purposes inconsistent with the intended purposes.

Assessment and analysis of whether each foreign government recipient is in compliance with section 620I of the Foreign Assistance Act of 1961, and whether such recipient has fully cooperated with United States Government efforts and United States Government-supported international efforts to provide humanitarian assistance in an area of armed conflict where the recipient country is using such defense articles and, as appropriate, defense services:

The Government of Nigeria (GON) permits humanitarian aid and access in garrison towns that are secure. The military mandates the use of escorts for humanitarian convoys travelling to unsafe areas when GON resources have been available. Humanitarian actors lacked access outside these areas due to insecurity and resource constraints. Negotiating humanitarian access with organized armed groups is criminalized under Nigerian law. The government in Borno State is keen to relocate internally displaced persons (IDPs). Some of the relocations led to IDPs living in areas that are insecure and/or inaccessible to humanitarian actors. USG-supported humanitarian partners are unable to implement certain programs outside of government-controlled areas in Borno State.

The USG assesses that the Nigerian government's posture on humanitarian access is not arbitrary but is a result of complex security threats and dangers posed to implementing partners and a lack of capacity to improve security. Any implementing partner that tries to go beyond the safe zones runs a high risk of kidnapping or death.

Somalia

Assessment of credible reports or allegations that certain defense articles and, as appropriate, defense services, have been used in a manner not consistent with international law, including international humanitarian law; such assessment shall include any determinations, if they can reasonably be made, as to whether use has occurred in a manner not consistent with international law, and if so, whether the recipient country has pursued appropriate accountability; and a description of the procedures used to make the assessments:

During the reporting period, there were credible reports of potential IHL and IHRL violations by government security forces in Somalia. The State Department's 2023 Country Reports on Human Rights Practices document credible reports of arbitrary or unlawful killings, including extrajudicial killings as well as the use of torture and other cruel, inhuman, or degrading treatment or punishment, and sexual violence.

The United Nations Assistance Mission in Somalia (UNSOM) reported state security personnel killed 61 civilians between February and October 2023. According to media reports, federal government soldiers killed 14 civilians during daily security-related activities between August and October. Nine perpetrators were arrested, prosecuted, and sentenced. NGOs also documented credible reports of government officials detaining terrorism suspects for prolonged periods and torturing them while in custody. Government security forces, including the National Intelligence and Security Agency and the Puntland Intelligence Agency, reportedly threatened, beat, and forced detainees to confess to crimes. There were reports of rape and sexual abuse by government agents. State security forces and affiliated militias reportedly operated with impunity, due to clan protection of perpetrators and weak government capacity and will to hold the guilty to account. While some military and police personnel accused of abuses were arrested and prosecuted, not all faced charges or were punished.

The sole recipient of NSM-20 covered defense articles in Somalia is the Somali National Army (SNA) Danab Brigade. The U.S. Government provides lethal assistance to this U.S.-funded, trained, and mentored brigade. The purpose of this U.S. assistance is to make the brigade capable of sustaining professional infantry forces proficient in counterterrorism operations. The brigade operates at the direction of the Chief of Defense Force and in coordination with the Federal Member States' security chief to counter al-Shabaab and ISIS-Somalia efforts to destabilize Somalia. The U.S. Government has direct insight into the Danab Brigade's use of covered defense articles and there is no information to indicate covered defense articles have been used by the partner in a manner inconsistent with international law.

Since 2021, and projected to continue through 2026, the Department of Defense has worked with the Somali Ministry of Defense and SNA leadership on development of an operational law training program for SNA legal advisors, integration of trained legal advisors into key aspects of military planning, and development of operational control mechanisms (Rules of Engagement/Rules for Use of Force/Civilian Harm Mitigation procedures) that reinforce adherence to the law of armed conflict and IHRL. DoD plans to assist with implementation of a table-top exercise to facilitate integration of identified SNA legal advisors with Danab commanders.

Assessment and analysis of (1) any credible reports indicating that the use of such defense articles has been found to be inconsistent with established best practices for mitigating civilian harm, and (2) the extent to which efforts to induce effective implementation of such civilian harm mitigation best practices have been incorporated into the relevant United States security assistance program; and a description of the procedures used to make the assessments:

Danab intake and basic training is conducted by State Department-funded mentors and includes extensive training on human rights and international humanitarian law. Following Danab basic training, soldiers are mentored by State Department-funded contractors and advised by U.S. military personnel who reinforce best practices for mitigating civilian harm, including measures implemented in response to the Department of Defense's CHMR-AP. Within the DoD-funded Danab support, mandatory training on civilian harm mitigation is annually conducted with the DIILS. Higher levels of DoD-funded training are also required when specific lethal items are provided to the partner nation.

Description of any known occurrences of such defense articles not being received by the recipient foreign government that is the intended recipient, or

being misused for purposes inconsistent with the intended purposes, and a description of any remedies undertaken:

The USG is not aware of defense articles covered under NSM-20 not being received by the intended foreign government recipient and/or being misused for purposes inconsistent with the intended purposes.

Assessment and analysis of whether each foreign government recipient is in compliance with section 620I of the Foreign Assistance Act of 1961, and whether such recipient has fully cooperated with United States Government efforts and United States Government-supported international efforts to provide humanitarian assistance in an area of armed conflict where the recipient country is using such defense articles and, as appropriate, defense services:

The Danab Brigade has facilitated USG-supported international efforts to provide humanitarian assistance in Somalia by working to eliminate the threat posed by al-Shabaab, a terrorist organization that has in the past worked to stymie the provision of U.S. humanitarian assistance to the Somali people.

Ukraine

Assessment of credible reports or allegations that certain defense articles and, as appropriate, defense services, have been used in a manner not consistent with international law, including international humanitarian law; such assessment shall include any determinations, if they can reasonably be made, as to whether use has occurred in a manner not consistent with international law, and if so, whether the recipient country has pursued appropriate accountability; and a description of the procedures used to make the assessments:

Since the beginning of Russia's full-scale invasion, the United States has committed more than $50.2 billion in security assistance to Ukraine. The Government of Ukraine is aware of the challenges they would face for any derogatory information implicating Ukraine's misuse of U.S.-provided defense articles.

The State Department's 2023 Country Reports on Human Rights Practices document credible reports of arbitrary detention and enforced disappearance of civilians, as well as torture or cruel, inhuman, or degrading treatment or punishment by government security forces and government-supported armed groups. The United Nations Human Rights Council Commission of Inquiry, media reporting, and nongovernmental organizations documented numerous incidents of alleged IHL and IHRL violations by state armed groups in 2023 and 2024.

According to the State Department's 2023 Country Reports on Human Rights Practices, the UN Office of the High Commissioner for Human Rights (OHCHR) documented 75 cases of arbitrary detention of civilians by law enforcement or armed forces, some of which the report stated amounted to enforced disappearance. There were also reports that law enforcement and military officials abused and, at times, tortured persons in custody to obtain confessions, usually related to alleged collaboration with Russia. Though the accused officials were sometimes charged with exceeding authority under martial law and/or sentenced to imprisonment, the government often did not take adequate steps to identify and punish officials who may have committed abuses during the reporting period.

Credible reports, including from the United Nations Human Rights Council Commission of Inquiry, also document potential IHRL violations by members of the Security Service of Ukraine (SBU). For example, SBU officers arrested and beat a man suspected of being a spy for Russia in March 2023 in Odesa Province. They kicked him and beat him with a rifle butt while asking him to confess that he was a spy. The victim reported he was requested to sign documents indicating he was a spy and threatened with further beatings in case of refusal. The Commission found, in that case, that the perpetrators had committed torture and arrested the victim arbitrarily, in violation of IHRL. Additionally, members of the SBU reportedly engaged in targeted killings of Ukrainian citizens believed to be supporting Russia. In March 2024, Lt General Vasili Malyuk, the director of the SBU, remarked during a broadcast on Ukraine's national television that the SBU engaged in an assassination campaign directed at "very many" individuals accused of war crimes and orchestrating attacks against Ukrainian citizens. Malyuk spoke of the killing of Ukraine-born Vladlen Tatarsky, a Kremlin propagandist and Ilya Kyva, a former Ukrainian parliament member. Kyva spoke out against Ukrainian independence and was considered a traitor by Kyiv before he was shot dead near Moscow in December of 2023. Sources within the SBU had previously told several outlets that the service was responsible for the killing.

Ukraine has undertaken a variety of efforts to implement its obligations under IHL. Ukraine has implemented a domestic requirement for members of the Armed Forces of Ukraine to understand and comply with IHL, as well as procedures for implementation. Ukraine has also taken steps to disseminate information regarding IHL, including IHL in military training and developing reference publications, memos, and videos on IHL compliance.

The Government of Ukraine has demonstrated a commitment to respect its obligations under IHL, to fully investigate any allegations of violations or abuses committed by its forces, and has been engaged in an effort to improve its program of training on IHL. Ukraine employs military lawyers, and Ukraine has domestic law that can be used to ensure accountability for violations committed by members of its armed forces. Ukrainian leaders have also fostered a command climate emphasizing the importance of complying with IHL.

A critical element of Ukraine's National Anti-Corruption Strategy is "ensuring effective state control over the observance by public servants of the rules of ethical conduct," including adherence to IHL. Minister of Defense Umerov has conveyed in multilateral forums like the Ukraine Defense Contact Group (UDCG) and bilateral engagements with U.S. and international counterparts his focus on the ethical use of partner provisioned security assistance and defense articles.

Assessment and analysis of (1) any credible reports indicating that the use of such defense articles has been found to be inconsistent with established best practices for mitigating civilian harm, and (2) the extent to which efforts to induce effective implementation of such civilian harm mitigation best practices have been incorporated into the relevant United States security assistance program; and a description of the procedures used to make the assessments:

The Ukrainian military is working (with U.S. assistance) to improve and follow best practices in use of force and civilian protection.

Description of any known occurrences of such defense articles not being received by the recipient foreign government that is the intended recipient, or being misused for purposes inconsistent with the intended purposes, and a description of any remedies undertaken:

The USG is not aware of defense articles covered under NSM-20 not being received by the intended foreign government recipient and/or being misused for purposes inconsistent with the intended purposes.

Assessment and analysis of whether each foreign government recipient is in compliance with section 620I of the Foreign Assistance Act of 1961, and whether such recipient has fully cooperated with United States Government efforts and United States Government-supported international efforts to provide humanitarian assistance in an area of armed conflict where the recipient country is using such defense articles and, as appropriate, defense services:

The Government of Ukraine has facilitated the delivery of U.S. humanitarian assistance, and humanitarians have not experienced systemic delays or obstructions. While there are access constraints to the delivery of humanitarian assistance in Ukraine, these instances are driven by the Government of Russia's active hostilities near frontline areas. Humanitarian organizations are operating in extremely difficult environments facing security concerns due to Russia's refusal to participate in the humanitarian de-confliction system.

The UN Office for the Coordination of Humanitarian Affairs reported as recently as December 2023 that visa delays, visa denials, bureaucratic, and administrative challenges with the Government of Ukraine delayed or otherwise negatively impacted aid delivery. However, appropriate ministries within the Government of Ukraine are actively engaged with the UN Resident and Humanitarian Coordinator in Ukraine on reducing or eliminating these limited issues.